M000045002

Forward

"If we are going to succeed in this life, we must shine the light in the darkest corners of our heart, mind, and soul. Glenis has done this in life and is willing to share the light with us. As you read this book, you will transform your life and improve the lives of some very special people who need our help."

Jim Stovall
Bestselling Author of The Ultimate Gift

Dedication to my Family & Friends

My ultimate Gratitude is my relationship with Jesus Christ my Lord, Savior and my God. After Him is my husband, Corey, and our nine amazing children - the four alive and the five in Heaven.

Corey, you are the sexiest piece of flesh, and I am proud to call you the man of my dreams. Without your love and support this book would still be a thought in my mind. Thank you, honey, for helping me push to reach my dreams.

Vanessa, JR, Daniel & Joy I am so grateful and thankful to God for allowing me to watch the miracle you all have become. You are all perfect in every way and I get to stand in eternal gratitude as I watch you all. May you live your life in complete Gratitude and live as if you are a special gift. You are my greatest and best gifts. I am eternally grateful He chose you all to bless me!

DC, Valentina, Daniel's future wife & Joy's future husband, I love you all. My prayers of Gratitude brought you all into my children's lives. You were covered in prayer years before you ever met the kids. I love you as if you were my own. May you all pass down the inheritance I leave to you all: allow Gratitude to transform your life forever as it has mine.

Life at times seems hard but God is extremely faithful and good. Allow Him to give you the 20/20 vision of Gratitude Transformation. When you pass stories down to the next generation talk about all of it, yes; but translate every story with the happy ending of Gratitude Transformation. God has a plan and a purpose for all He has allowed. May you find the gratitude in all of life's circumstances.

To my delicious Glamkids - David Josiah, Isabella Joy, Lilly, and Ella - you make my world perfect just thinking of you. David Josiah, you are the king of my heart and the first of many grandkids. I love your curly hair and your kind, quiet spirit. You pushed me to love and be present like no other. Isabella Joy, you are my princess and I bow to your love for me. You are my Anna and Elsa combined. I love you beyond life. I promise you Grandma is going to buy a second home close to you so I can come back and forth to see you grow up. Lilly, your happy, kind, beautiful face on its own is enough for me to open up my eyes to gratitude. Ella, you, are probably the one and only Galindo child, as far as Daddy thinks, but I will love you like you were ten little Galindos running around.

To my mother, Alma, who predominantly speaks Spanish - Mami, aunque mides meno de cinco pies tu corazon es gigante. Mami, gracias por educarme en el amor. Mami, que te digo. Eres un tronco que dejara raices por eternidad.This all translates to - Mom, although you are less than five feet, your heart is giant. Mom, thank you for bringing me up in love. Mom, you are the epitome of gratitude.

To my eight siblings, and possibly nine if the man who recently showed up is my father's son, I thank all of you. We officially have three boys named Juan, after my late father. Although they are all from different mothers, we are joined together in love and deep gratitude. God sure gave me a dysfunctional bunch, but I could not be more grateful. I fit right into this family. Thank you, mi familia. God blessed me with all of you, and I can't thank Him enough.

To my friends who are like family to me, I love you. You each have changed my life and allowed my Gratitude Transformation to evolve. From the most successful to the homeless, I have welcomed all of you into my space. I am forever grateful for your own stories of Gratitude Transformation.

Dedication to the People of the Bahamas

For a very long time I was so afraid of launching this book. I was frightened by what others might think about my story. But, after the most recent hurricane, Hurricane Dorian, devastated parts of the Bahamas, I knew it was time to launch this book so that much of the proceeds from the sale of this book could go toward helping the Bahamians impacted by Hurricane Dorian.

One day I was arguing with God. Yes, I do that sometimes. I argued with him about the timing of launching the book, and He told me now was the right time. I dropped into a spirit of gratitude and began praising and thanking Him. I told Him I wanted to give but didn't know how. My husband and I set up our gym, Fitness for Everybody, as a drop-off center for items to be sent to the Bahamas. We've even hosted events there to raise funds for the island. I still felt like there was more I could and should do. That's when I heard God loud and clear, "I spared Floridians, did I not? It is because of Gratitude

Transformation that you all should give, especially you, Glenis!" I said, "Excuse me?" I was on the floor after that. God then said, "Why don't you give of what you have?" I said, "God, if I make another post about giving, people are going to block me on Facebook."

Back and forth I went with God. He said, "You always need translation don't you, girl?" I said, "Yes Jesus! Please translate. I don't speak English that well." He said, "NO! This is what I mean. Launch your book and I will use it to transform your life and the lives of many." I was determined to fight God on this. "No, I don't like that translation. My kids can publish that kind of book when I am gone." He continued, "I allowed this to take place so that the world would be united by Gratitude Transformation. They will see clearly a hurricane coming to Florida and then shifting and staying in an area where there is great need. The world is going to come together to make the Bahamas strong again. You can be part of that."

"Okay, Lord! I will do it." As much as I wanted to keep fighting the Lord, I relented. He began to show me how many times my life has been impacted by hurricanes and how my life has been changed forever because of them. I was a teenager in the Dominican Republic in 1979 when Hurricane David came through and caused 1200 people to die, left many homeless and millions of dollars in damage to the island. We were spending the weekend at my Tia Lillian's home, and I was afraid that we were going to die there. My Tia (aunt) shared with me how, at six years old, her, my mother's and my other aunt's life were changed because of a hurricane that hit in Tamboril, a side country where people were very poor. When my grandmother left my grandfather, he was left to be a single father. He built a small home in back of his father's house, and that is where my mother and aunts stayed while he would go to work two hours away. The house locked from the outside so the little girls couldn't get out at night. When the hurricane came through in 1943, he could not get back to the house in time and no one remembered the three little girls trapped in the house in the backyard. My Tia Lillian was the oldest. My aunt was four and my mother was a year old. Tia

Lillian told us how she banged on the door and walls until her hands bled. She found peace in the middle of the storm and knew someone would save them. She was persistent in trying to get help to rescue them she said not so much for herself, but for her two little sisters left in her care. Her tenacity caused them to be saved from the house before it was destroyed.

When she told me that story in 1979, I knew that I wanted to help victims of hurricanes. I have since then experienced several other hurricanes that were life changing - 2004, 2017, 2018, and 2019. The one in 2017 was the most defining one of them all, and you will come to discover why as you read more of my story. The hurricane of 2017 changed the entire trajectory of my life, as I am sure Hurricane Dorian will do for the people of the Bahamas. I pray my story will help shift them into a place of Gratitude rather than victimhood, and that they see how God can take destruction and turn it into destiny.

My Pinky Promise to My Readers

My hope is that by reading *The Gratitude Transformation* you will find more Joy, be more in the present, be more at peace, and be more successful in any area you choose; whether it is your finances, your fitness, your relationships, your spiritual life, your contributions, or all of the above. I think there is abundance all around me, so I choose every one of these areas. How about you?

Deep down I believe we are all looking for higher results in our lives, and we struggle as to how to bring this about. The answer has always been there. It is also FREE. The answer is GRATITUDE.

Gratitude Morning Routine

If you start your day with implementing a Gratitude routine, I believe this small change can change your life drastically. Your morning Gratitude routine will feel as if you are downloading a daily dose of happiness, purpose, passion, joy, serenity, compassion, and love. Having morning routines has changed my life for the past twenty-seven years. Introducing my special time of Gratitude as the first and last thing I do as I wake up and as I go to sleep has revolutionized my life. The way we start our day is sometimes the way we finish our day. I believe the way we finish our day also impacts the next day. We get so much more done if we start a morning routine, but a Gratitude morning and evening routine gets us The Gratitude Transformation.

Anything you and I do consistently becomes our lifestyle. At the core, I believe we are all looking to live more fulfilling lives. If you had asked me a few years ago if Joy, presence, abundance, peace, and serenity were important in my life I would have said.... NOPE, not on my agenda. On my to-do list you would have found other things that I considered more important. Raising children as a single mom without killing them or myself, paying off debt, helping addicts in their journey to sobriety, helping my clients, saving the world...I thought I needed to be superwoman for people to like me or accept me. I am Grateful to report my approval addiction has also lessened after introducing Gratitude in my life.

What changed, you might ask? The simple answer is - EVERYTHING!

Once I chose Gratitude, I attracted amazing people into my life. I went on the express train of abundance instead of the local train of regrets. I was not aware that I could choose my own ride. Gratitude, which is still a free feeling available to all of us, was my answer to a happier, better, more meaningful life. Once I fully stepped into Gratitude, I was able to accomplish my dreams in a very short amount of time. I even went beyond accomplishing my dreams. I started going back to every trial, every tribulation that I had experienced, and I was able to redefine them from a place of love, acceptance, and Gratitude. I forgave me, and I learned to forgive others. As I let go of the old stories and stepped into Gratitude, I was able to love and appreciate me and others so much more. I could not understand what had happened. It was like I finally opened the jail cell. I felt so free. My desire for you is that you have the same experience. The solutions are always inside of use if we get quiet and see the world from our new Eyes of Gratitude.

I wrote this book to help you do the same and live what I call *The Gratitude Transformation*. As you read my story and share in the trials and challenges I had to overcome to get to a place of Gratitude, my prayer is that you will see your life's challenges and trials as the starting point to shifting you from anger, frustration, and bitterness to a place of joy, excitement, and happiness for what's to come from your own Gratitude Transformation. I pinky promise you after you read my story, you will begin to see your own life from a new lens. It may seem strange that I can be grateful after what I've done and experienced. But Gratitude is a choice and I hope you, like me, choose it every day.

Introduction

Not everyone wants light shed on the dark spaces in their life - those spaces where we sweep things hoping no one will see them. That's not me! I appreciate the light because it's the only way I could get to the other side of my painful past.

When I made the decision to share my story, it wasn't initially easy. You see, for almost twenty years I've been trying to tell parts of this story. I never realized that God had to take me through a series of extreme events, even up until 2017, that would shake me to the core. It was because of it all that I was able to find gratitude in everything.

My walk through this life has been far from perfect. You would see me now and think I've always been this successful wife, mother, business owner with her life neatly put together. Definitely not the case!

I'm finally prepared to expose it all, shine the light so I can help you and so many others be set free to experience your own

Gratitude Transformation. Some of my story will be tough to read. Trust me! I lived it and then relived it by writing this book. But, in it you will be able to see why I am so thankful to my Heavenly Father, Jesus Christ, for allowing me to bear it all. I am transformed by his grace and eternally grateful that I get the chance to tell you my story, my way.

Chapter 1
Mean

To say my grandmother was mean would be an understatement. Mean is when someone says something unkind to you. Mean is the kid who knocks another child's ice cream cone to the ground for no reason. Mean is when you walk up to two of your "friends" and invite one of them to your party without inviting the other. Those might be some of the things you think about when you hear the word "mean." Well, to me, those things would be considered nice compared to what I endured living with my grandmother.

I was born in the Dominican Republic. A mixed-race family with a grandmother who didn't like me because I looked and leaned toward my dad's side of the family.

He was dark-skinned, something she hated. She looked down on me and treated me like dirt because of it. The abuses that began in my life started before my earliest memories. My dad died when I was three, and immediately my mother was a single mom trying to figure out life all over again. My mother did everything she could to provide and take care of us, but it wasn't easy.

We had been living in my grandfather's home for a few years after my dad died. My mom finally moved on and got a new boyfriend. When she got pregnant by her boyfriend, her stepmother wasn't happy about that. Being unmarried and pregnant was a no-no in my family. So, my mother was asked to leave the house. Since she didn't have money to find a place of her own, she sent me and my sister to live with our grandmother while she moved to New York to follow her baby's father and try to make a better life for herself and us.

Not only was I sexually abused at the age of three by my cousin after my dad died, but from six to ten, living at my grandmother's house, I faced unbelievable prejudice and abuse. She hated my skin color. Made me wish I was fair-skinned like my mother. If she could bleach my skin just short of killing me, I believe she would have. Instead of affirming me like a grandmother should, she degraded me with her words and the vile looks she would throw my way. All this because of my skin color.

She despised my father and made it clear through her words and actions that she didn't like me either. Can you imagine not feeling loved by the person responsible for caring for you? My mother had placed me in her protection, yet my grandmother was the main one I needed protection from.

She was so abusive and made fun of my hair. She yanked my hair so hard I ended up with bumps on my skull. I remember getting lice once, and she washed my hair with rat poison. My hair was kinky curly, so she would straighten my hair with an iron. Literally ironing my hair like she was ironing a shirt. Some would say she didn't know any better. She did. That made it even more hurtful.

I never yelled at her. Never called her outside her name. Never treated my grandmother with anything but respect. That's how you were to treat your "Abuela." Until one day, my sister and I were so tired of the way she treated me, we threw a plastic lizard at her. She was terrified of lizards, and we knew it. Abuela had a mild heart attack and went to the hospital. When she came back, I was severely beaten.

I couldn't take it any longer. At ten years old at a Christmas gathering I told my family I had to leave. If I didn't, I was either going to kill her or kill myself. I did not want to, but I would if I had to endure any further abuse from her. God heard my prayers. Or so I thought. I moved to my grandfather's house from ten to thirteen, where I was abused by uncles and aunts while living there. I couldn't catch a break. I needed my mother. During those seven years, our mother was still very present in our lives and did everything she could to get me and my sister to be in the States with her. She had already moved to the United States and went through painstaking challenges to get her green card to no avail. In the process of trying to get her green card, she was lied to and her money was stolen. Anything that could deter her from getting her green card would happen, and she was frustrated. She ended up marrying a US citizen and was able to get her green card by the time I turned thirteen. My sister and I then moved to New York to live with her.

I wanted the move to be a turning point for me. I wanted to erase every memory of the emotional, physical, and sexual abuses I suffered while living in my grandmother's house and grandfather's house. But by thirteen, the pain was embedded in my memory bank and didn't want to set me free.

There was a time I wanted to tell my mother the things happening to me at

Abuela's house. I even learned how to write by writing down all of the abuses I was suffering. Abuela never mailed my letters. She kept them, making me think all those years that my mother didn't care. It never made sense to me that she was so hateful. Her hate for me eventually turned into my own self-hatred.

Here I was living in New York City, the place where dreams were made. But I was broken with no hope. What do you do when the pain of your life engulfs you never allowing you to know peace? For me, as a young teen, I turned to drugs praying to find peace in the midst of the swelling pain. I was a hope-to-die drug addict and lived that way for fourteen years.

Crazy enough, I graduated with honors from school and graduated at fifteen and a half. I got a scholarship to go to NYU but decided to go to a business college instead. I lived a double life. At thirteen I started doing drugs. At sixteen I became a topless dancer and had my first abortion - the first of five abortions during my 14-year drug addiction.

I lived in a chokehold from all the years of never feeling good enough. Always seeing my mean grandmother's face staring at me telling me, "You're ugly." "You're too dark." "¡Nunca serás nada!" You'll never be anything. That was one of her favorite things to say to me. Her words stayed with me all throughout those fourteen years, until with one prayer, my Heavenly Father set me free from my self-deprecating lifestyle. I was on the path to my gratitude transformation.

Scripture to meditate on:

"He sent His word and healed them, And rescued them from their destruction" (Psalms 107:20 AMP).

Homework:

Think about the situations in your life that have been the most difficult for you to handle. There's a simple exercise I used to help me let all of it go. I call it *Transforming Blame into Gratitude.* I want you to do this exercise so you, too, can release the bad and see the good God can make from it.

1. Write out three of your major life challenges.

2. Write out everything you can be grateful for about the situations.

3. Call or mail a letter to the person who hurt you. Don't blame them. Thank them.

The more committed you are to giving up the blame, the less power your challenges have over you. The more grateful you become, the faster you set yourself free. Your gratitude transformation may also set your "abusers" free, too.

Chapter 2
Addiction & Love

When you look back at your life, and you think about the people, places, things that have opened you up to the person you are today, do you smile? Are you grateful that God chose you to go through the trauma, the pain, the hurt, the destruction in order to come out whole on the other side? Today, I can truly say that I am. Now, don't get me wrong! It wasn't at all easy to get to a place of gratitude. I spent far too many days and nights strung out and high trying to block out the memories of my past.

"Lord, I am an addict. I need you to take this addiction from me now." I remember the first time I prayed those words out loud in an effort to rid myself of the drug addiction that nearly destroyed everything in me. Fourteen years I spent bound to drugs, addicted to pain, walking in fear. Hopeless. That's what I was, hopeless.

For much of my earlier life, I lived hopelessly addicted. I was dating a man, Marco, that would eventually become my first husband. I knew he wasn't good for me, but as an an addict I didn't care if he was good for me. It was more about him just being there. I remember the years 1988 and 1989 so vividly because during that timeframe, I had gotten pregnant three times by Marco. I terminated all three pregnancies because I was ashamed and embarrassed. I was raised Catholic, and to be pregnant and unmarried was a grave sin. Feeling guilty over the abortions, but also not wanting to have his child at the same time, it seemed like if he looked at me, I would get pregnant. I had ravaged my body so badly from the drugs and abortions that the doctor told me I would never have a child. I ended up getting pregnant again that year and decided to keep my last pregnancy. Marco and I ended up getting married April 7, 1989, and our daughter, Vanessa, was born February 1, 1990. My God! Do you see how He can bring victory even in the midst of a lose-lose situation? The doctor had counted me out, but God never counted me out.

On Halloween of 1991, Marco and I had gone out to party because, that next day, he was supposed to be turning himself into the police for a previous crime he'd committed. While out, he thought I was flirting with another man. He got so upset and ended up dragging me down the stairs. Needless to say, I was happy he was going to prison the next day. I needed to get my life together without him. While he was imprisoned, I found out he had been unfaithful to me when he was home. I was infuriated and began dating other men. He found out and had his previous ex-wife to spy on me and provide him with the proof of my infidelity. He wanted nothing to do with me after that. So, the week before I came to fully know Jesus for myself, I remember driving from the prison where he was at and just crying out to God saying, "Please! God, if you are up there, I don't care what happens to me, just save my little girl." I was crying so desperately that I had to pull the car over to avoid getting into an accident with Vanessa in the car. That drive was one of the turning points in my relationship with Christ. I ended up giving my life to Christ that next week on November 19, 1991. I began to see the Father's hand at work, and that my addiction would soon be stripped from me. I was about to be stripped of co-dependency. I was about to embark on the next stage of my life. A life where blessings and mercy would overflow, but so would trials and turmoil.

Vanessa was born blind in one eye. At the age of three, the doctors began treating her eye condition. I was devastated and filled with remorse for my years of drug abuse and addiction before and during my pregnancy. "This is my fault!" I would scream this at the top of my lungs each time I went to God in prayer about my baby girl. I cried out to God daily for Him to heal her and that I would do anything for Him if He did what I knew only He could do. Have you ever tried to negotiate with God, tried to get what you needed from Him but not really sure you were ready to give up anything in return? It's a good thing God doesn't negotiate with us. He will either bless us right there in the midst of our mess or take some time before He shows up to do the miraculous. Well, He took His time! Ten years later, Vanessa was freed from the blindness in her eye. Hallelujah! I can shout now, but that ten-year waiting period was nothing to play with. It was hard. It was grueling. I stayed on my knees so much I got rug burn on my knees. I couldn't even see my way to Gratitude during that time. "God, take my sight instead." "My child is innocent. She doesn't deserve this." Over and over I went to God with this. I begged and pleaded...and I waited. Vanessa had to wear contact lenses at three years old, and we would have to patch her strong eye in order to strengthen the weak one. She was teased as a child. Other children taunted her because of the patch or when they saw the cataract she was born with and eventually had removed by the age of three. Unless you've been through it, you can't begin to imagine the agony of a parent having to straight-jacket their child to put a contact in their eye. It would take three adults about one hour in the morning and another hour at night to get the contact in and out of her eye. I needed God to heal that thing. That thing that was in her eye because of that thing in me...my addiction, or so I thought. I watched her suffer physically as I suffered in my soul.

The word of the Lord says in John 9: 1-3 AMP, "While He was passing by, He noticed a man blind [who had been] from birth. His disciples asked Him, 'Rabbi (Teacher), who sinned, this man or his parents, that he would be born blind?' Jesus answered, 'Neither this man nor his parents sinned, but it was so that the works of God might be displayed and illustrated in him."

All that time I spent living with guilt and shame, believing my addiction was what had caused my daughter's eye condition. No! God needed me to recognize that His works would be displayed and illustrated in Vanessa. My addiction had nothing to do with what God needed to do to Vanessa in order to birth through her who she is today. Because of what she endured, she is so compassionate and understanding of others' pain. She is kind and giving. She has chosen to love all that God continues to bring into her life. What I thought was because of my addiction truly was all about the love that God wanted to display through her. I say to her all the time, "Mija (daughter), I am so proud of you. I'm not sure you are mine, sweetie." She laughs like only she can.

As messed up as I was before I knew Christ, I became another person. I opened my home to women who were addicts just like me. I taught them to work. They took my company from a one-person company to a booming company with twenty-three employees. I had one of the biggest restoration companies in California. I had a warehouse. Most of those employees were recovering addicts. I had eleven people living with me. The Lord allowed me to take the mess of my life and turn it around to be able to teach and train people. I had most of those people work with me for a year or two and then I would send them out. I would send them out to open their own companies and I would hire new people. I did that for quite some time. I realized that during the time I had spent using drugs, I developed my customer service and business skills. Yes, it was a horrible way to learn. Yet, I am grateful I was able to take those skills and turn them into something positive, something that would give God glory. A thriving business.

Marco had gotten out of prison less than two years later. After he got out, the doctors again told us that we would not get pregnant and that I could not have children. They said I had messed up my body beyond repair and that maybe if I went into treatment, maybe I could have a child. With Marco standing next to me, I told the doctor, "No. God delivered me. God took away drugs in a second with a simple prayer. God is going to give me a son and his name is Marco Jr." I went home and I painted a room blue and I said, "Marco is coming." Everybody thought I was crazy. I bought a crib for

Marco Jr. I bought everything a boy would need. Everything. And three months later, I was pregnant with Marco Jr. I didn't do a pregnancy test. I just knew. God showed me I was pregnant.

Three pregnancy tests later, because my husband didn't believe, he said, "Well, we'll just go to the doctor and do the blood test." Confirmed, I was pregnant. Even the lady that eventually did the ultrasound, she said of my account of the day I got pregnant, "In 16 years doing this job, I have never seen that where someone is right on the date." I said, "That day I didn't make it up, God showed me that day." And Marco Jr., born November 1993, is 25-years old today. He's an incredible young man. He's a power-lifter. He's married with his own child on the way, and I couldn't be prouder.

Not only did God give me that son, but God then gave me Daniel. With Daniel, I went through a lot during that pregnancy. That's when the Nextel phones came out and I thank God for them because I was able to run a crew of twenty-three employees and a whole bunch of subcontractors doing insurance work, from a mattress in my warehouse and a two-way radio. We were able to build houses during the time that I was bedridden. I started getting contractions from Daniel the minute that I was pregnant and that's how I knew I was pregnant. I was separated from the kids' dad. Marco Sr. and I spent more time apart than we did together.

Our children are three years apart, all of them, because I would get pregnant, he would leave, be with other women and then he would come back. I would get pregnant; he would leave, and the cycle continued. With Daniel, we had gone out for my birthday, did a little too much celebrating, and I got pregnant. There was an evangelist that came to a conference that the church did. It was their yearly conference and this man came from another part of the world. He said, "The woman that the doctors said that she would never have a child, I want that woman to come forward. I want that woman to come to the altar." I remember being so scared because I didn't want to go up there and everybody that went to the church that knew my story out of thousands of people, they all kept on looking at me and I felt their eyes on me. Eventually, someone said, "That's you Glenis." I went up there and the man was preaching out of the book of Daniel. My son was going to be named Joshua, but that night I made the decision that my son would be named Daniel. God had a plan for Daniel. Daniel was going to bring me closer to God than any other child I would ever have and that's exactly what has happened.

From the time I got pregnant with Daniel, I began having contractions. I had to be checked every day because the contractions were so consistent. September 5, 1996, I was taking Vanessa and Marco Jr. to register for school. My contractions were coming every three minutes. I went for my checkup and the nurse discovered that he was fully crowned. I didn't even know because nothing felt different to me. I was already eight centimeters dilated. Another nurse came into the room to take my kids out and by the time the other nurse put me on the gurney, BOOM - Daniel was born two minutes later. He came so quickly that we actually nicknamed him Daniel "Boom."

Daniel is so different from all my other children. Because of how he came into the world, I believe he will get a special crown in Heaven. Everything he sets his hands to will prosper. He will move swiftly through life but be able to take in the small lessons God wants him to learn along the way. He is a young man who has his own way of doing life. You tell him, "Go right," he goes left. But that's what makes him so amazing to me. I have learned to pray and be a better human being because of Daniel, and I thank him because he has helped me do my own Parental Gratitude Transformation.

Marco Sr. and I were already separated, but I found myself pregnant again. He was living with another woman who he had been with for eight years. At that point, I had had many venereal diseases except AIDS, by the grace of God. I was praying and I was trusting God. I fasted twice a week, I prayed, I covered that man with prayer and asked God to save him. Nothing. Nothing. Eventually, I just filed for a divorce because I said, "God, that's it. I'm done. I can't take this anymore. I can't do this anymore. I thought you were not going to give me more than I could handle, but I just can't do this anymore."

I turned the business over to Marco Sr. because he said the reason why he wasn't with me was because I wanted to be the man in the house. I turned a thriving business over into his hands when I was pregnant with our youngest, Joy. Within three months, we owed money, and we couldn't pay utilities—I couldn't believe he took a business that brought in thousands of dollars monthly and he had gambled it away in three months.

Let me tell you, learning about yourself is hard work. Going through the things I went through during my addiction taught me a lot about myself and what I did and did not deserve, especially when it came to love and men. I stayed in a very unhealthy marriage for many years because of being afraid. Marco Sr. would say to me, "Who is going to want you with four kids?" "You are a dirty black woman, and nobody will want you." I believed those words for many years and failed at respecting myself as a woman. I am extremely grateful that eventually I got over his words and my fears. I decided that if I was going to fail, I would fail forward and not care if I messed up my face from the fall. I told myself, "Glenis, if you need to raise these kids alone, that is a great honor." My mother had raised four girls on her own and she survived, so I knew I could do it too.

I no longer wanted to be co-dependent. During my years of addiction, co-dependency was one of the most destructive behaviors I dealt with. I remember getting divorced and the following Sunday the kids' dad took them for the day, and I got some time alone. I drove to the beach and started crying. I couldn't figure out what I wanted to do with my life. I had spent so much time pleasing my ex-husband and trying to figure out what made him happy that I forgot about how to be happy for myself. In recovery, they say co-dependent people are the kind of people who when they are on their death bed, they think of what could have made others happy instead of themselves. I was so consumed with the approval of men in my life that I forgot about living. My relationships were one-sided. You've been there, too, right? I had very few healthy relationships. If a man actually loved and cared for me, I would run him off and out of my life. I was so comfortable in my dysfunction. Not only was I addicted to drugs, I was addicted to men who were one-sided in relationships...they took from me and never gave anything of substance - just like the drugs. I needed to stop with the co-dependency on everything and become fully dependent on God.

I learned for myself that when you're an addict, you want everything right then and there. You don't want to wait. You want what you want when you want it, and you don't care how you have to get it. We don't want to be in a waiting season; at least I didn't want to wait for Vanessa's healing. But, look at what waiting those ten years did for her and for me. Addiction will suck the life out of you. It will also expose you to who you really are, if you let it. I needed to know Glenis beyond the addiction. I needed God to expose me to ME - my future self - the one He was calling me to be outside of the drugs and abuse I had grown so accustomed to.

Are you ready to be exposed to YOU in order to get to your place of Gratitude?

Scripture to meditate on:
"Blessed is the man who walks not in the counsel of the wicked, nor stands in the way of sinners, not sits in the seat of scoffers; but his delights is in the law of the Lord, and on his law he meditates day and night. He is like a tree planted by streams of water that yields its fruit in its

season, and its leaf does not wither. In all that he does, he prospers" (Psalms 1:1-3 ESV).

Homework:

Think about the qualities in you, those negative aspects of your life, that others may see as bad, but you are Grateful for what that quality has done for you. For me, it was how I honed my business and customer service skills. For you, it may be something else. Write it out and profess to God that you will turn that thing around for your good and for His glory.

When you can identify those things in yourself that make you appear undesirable in man's eyes, God will clearly show you that you are still the apple of His eye. That will make you become addicted to his love and Grateful for who He has created you to be.

Chapter 3
Miracles

I remember when I was still married to Marco, a detective came to the door at eight o'clock in the morning after the kids had gone to school. Thank God for favor because Marco and I got arrested that morning, and our two older kids weren't there to witness it.

The detectives took me in because they said that I rented a car and never returned it. What?! I told the detectives, "Look, I have no reason to rent the sedan. I own two luxury cars that are paid for in my driveway. I have a home that has half a million dollars in equity. I owe $100,000. I have a successful business. There is no reason for me to rent a $15,000 car and not return it." They separated the two of us. They took me in one car and took him in another. After they ran my ex's record and realized the kind of man he was, they asked me, "Why are you with this man?" I said, "I'm a Christian. I'm praying for him to come to know Jesus and for his life to be turned around, and we have four children together. I was raised without a dad; I don't want my kids to be raised without their dad. I'm waiting on God to do what only God can do. I'm okay with waiting." They said he told them eventually that I had nothing to do with the car, that it was him and the girlfriend that rented the car. So, he got three different felonies that day. One for forgery. One for stealing the car and one for driving without a license. They let me go. As they were letting me go, a detective said, "You said you were a Christian and that you were praying for God to show you whether he is committing adultery or not. Well, we know he's living with another woman and he's been at that address for eight years, which is about ten minutes from your home. That's his address and that's where he lives," they slid the address across to me. He used to come home three or four days out of the week, and he would say he was in the casino. He had a gambling problem when I met him. It just escalated and it continued through the years. But when I finally filed for the divorce, it was because if I didn't then I was putting myself in a situation where I wasn't going to be able to take care of my children.

I was in the precinct for eight hours before they released me. I am eternally grateful that I never got a record and that they let me go because I wouldn't have been able to continue doing my job if I had a record. The minute I saw myself in a prison, I said, "If this man continues to live his life the way he's lived his life and I continue to enable him and allow him, then I won't be able to raise my children." That's when I knew I had to file for divorce.

One day in church, I said to my friend, Sandy, "I can't believe I'm pregnant." We didn't know whether I was having a boy or a girl. She passed me a note during service, and the note said, "Her name will be Joy, and she will be the Joy of the Lord." She named our daughter. And Joy has been nothing but a joy. I was 35 years old, and because of my age they had to do a test to make sure that Joy was healthy. The results were a little alarming - "abnormal" is what they said. She wasn't born with down-syndrome, but the genetics, the sixth chromosome is where the tenth should be, and the tenth where the sixth should be. But God!

I told that church and the people in that church whom became my family to pray, to fast with me and to trust God. When Joy was born, they tested Joy again and they said, "Yeah, for sure. She's going to be a special needs child." My pastor's wife, Mary Lou Aldaco, said, "Now that we know that she is special needs, now that we have the security, we have the proof, it's up to you Glenis. We can stop praying. We can stop fasting—it is up to you what you want us to do. We can allow God to do what God can do and He can do greater miracles now that we know. Or we can just stop." I said, "Please, don't stop."

Three months later, the specialist did another test and they didn't understand what had happened. This woman that was the genetics specialist said that she didn't know what happened and that I had to prepare myself because things could change, but that the tests were normal. Joy was tested at 6 months and again at a year, and it didn't affect her. They told me that when she became a teenager, I had to let her know that this could affect her children. I told the doctor I was not telling my daughter such things because I believe God had done the work. God healed my daughter the same way God healed me, and Joy is now 19 years old.

I understand what it means to experience miracles; I know from experience. As I was going through the worst time in my life and finally filed for the divorce, there was a widow in our church who needed a place to live. I was accustomed to letting people stay with me, so I offered for her to stay with me rather than having to relocate to live with her daughter. But this widow was different. The fire of God walked with her, and she fully brought

Him into my home when I needed Him the most. Sister Virginia opened up Heavenly realms when she prayed. Her special anointing to pray for the sick healed many souls. It was because of her that I learned to pray like never before. She had a powerful influence over my prayer life and taught me faith like no other. The holes in my soul soon began to heal because of the prayers she released over me and my home. Like my children, Sister Virginia was another miracle God designed specifically for me.

What are the miracles you know God designed just for you?

Scripture to meditate on:
"But Jesus looked at them and said to them, 'With men this is impossible, but with God all things are possible" (Matthew 19:26 NKJV).

Homework:

Grab your journal and write out the miracles you've witnessed in your life, or the life of your family, because of your prayers.

God is a miracle worker, and I experienced it for myself with my children, through my circumstances with Marco, and by the power of prayer. There are so many other miracles I could share with you, but it would take another book to share. Know that when you are in your darkest moments, God is always up to something. When it seems impossible, that's when He will send your miracle.

Chapter 4

Changed

I look at my life now and remember when I was so strung out on drugs, I couldn't see my way out. When God released me from the chokehold of drugs, co-dependency, low self-esteem, and so much more, I began to see how he was going to use me to help set others free. I realize now that God had to change me in order to use me, but I had to be a willing vessel He could work through.

After I moved to Florida when Joy was four, I began to do a lot of introspection and work on myself. I became part of a ministry called "Celebrate Recovery" where I more fully learned I was a co-dependent. I started seeing a therapist back in California and she recommended a book called Codependent No More by Melody Beattle. I sat down and read all 200 plus pages in one sitting. As I read, I kept saying, "That's me. That's me. That's me." Eventually, the pastor's wife in this new church I started attending, she was a biker - a tough lady, she had experienced an incredible transformation. She said to me, "Listen, I don't know how you have been guided in your old church, but you are going to a get a trophy in Heaven that the enemy never wanted you to have. You should have divorced that man years ago. What type of example are you setting for your kids - your daughters?" She said, "I really want you to pray and ask God to show you." That broke me down. I didn't want to be a bad example to my children. I wanted to be changed, transformed from the inside out.

Gratitude Transformation can happen once we understand that our circumstances do not need to break us; they can actually make us better human beings. It is up to us to allow those circumstances, struggles and mishaps to make us bitter or better. We get to choose. I look at my past now and feel a sense of gratitude that God would have seen fit to allow the difficulties to happen to me. They have made me stronger, wiser, more grateful, more mindful, more joyous, more accepting of myself and others. Most of all, they've made me a lot more fun to be around because I'm no longer miserable wallowing in self-pity from the pain of my past.

It's out of my own pain that I developed a passion for helping others, giving them a place to live, jobs to help sustain them and their family. I had to change in order to help change the lives of those God had assigned to me. This former addict has been able to speak to hundreds of people and affect hundreds of lives because of my story of hope, gratefulness and transformation. I've taken in so many people into my home when they needed a place to stay. My home has been a revolving door for former addicts, the hopeless and homeless who didn't have a place to lay their head. All of my ups and downs have made me who I am along this journey, and I love who I have chosen to be. I had to rise from the debris of my life, move away from those things that constantly reminded me of who I used to be, in order to see a shift happen in my life. I no longer question, "Why me?" But, rather, I say, "Why not me!" because I am grateful and thankful God chose me to walk out this life. With all of my struggles, He also gave me His strength. It's like He literally blew new life into my nostrils, opened up my mouth wide so I can proclaim His faithfulness and use my voice to help those feeling stuck in victim mode in their lives.

Anytime I am going through difficulty in my life, I think, "Yes, I went through what I went through in my marriage, but we're close friends today and we laugh about how he used to be. He was an addict, too. Except his vice was gambling. Funny that my father was a gambler, and the man I married turned out to be one, too. Marco would have gambled anything and everything because that's where he was at in life. He didn't know any better. He didn't have the capacity to do better, so I had to learn to let go of all the past hurt from my marriage. That was a part of my transformation process. To me, no matter what I've gone through, I use that - my marriage, the abuse, the addiction, as an opportunity to say, "Okay, I got over that. I went through that; therefore, I can get through this." This is the type of self-talk I give myself when reminding myself that I've been changed and set free from the tricks of the enemy.

The life I live today is totally unrecognizable from the one I was handed as a kid. I now have a new husband, Corey, who loves me to life. We are successful business owners who make it a priority to love God first, each other second, and our family third. We know in that order we can't get it wrong. I am forever grateful to God for my gratitude transformation in this area of my life. I had to be obedient and make the necessary changes to my life and lifestyle in order to experience the victory I have now.

When was the revelatory moment you realized God was showing you it was time to transform?

Scripture to meditate on:

"Therefore, if anyone is in Christ, he is a new creation; old things have passed away; behold, all things have become new" (2 Corinthians 5:17 NKJV).

Homework:

Get a flipchart and begin listing the things from your past (the remnants of your former self) that you want to erase and create something new about yourself. Once you've laid it all out on the flipchart, ask God to eradicate those negative memories of who you once were and replace them with new, positive images of who He has called you to be.

I am so grateful that He changed me, and if you fully surrender to Him, He will change your life, too. I wanted to experience a new life, a new lifestyle, a new mindset, and a new spiritual way of being. It took the troubles in my marriage and recognizing my codependency for me to see that I needed to transform. I needed to be a better version of myself. I needed to do a 180°, a complete about-face, to leave behind those things which were behind me. When living in gratitude transformation mode, it is your right to do the same thing, so you are no longer trapped in the bondage of your former life.

Chapter 5

Intentional Accidents Happen

Now, here I was transforming - becoming this new creation that God had awakened in me. I was riding the clouds of life with my amazing husband, my beautiful children and "glam-kids" (as I love to call my grandchildren). My business was flourishing. I was still serving God, helping people, and getting my physical body together once I had my spiritual and emotional life in order. Then...BAM! Life, as I had come to know it, was suddenly flipped upside down. Or, should I say my life ended on October 2, 2017...

There was devastation everywhere in the Florida Keys. I happened to be there right after the first Category 5 hurricane that caused forty-two billion dollars in damage in the Atlantic. I spent the day talking to people and driving around to see the damage for the first time. It was completely overwhelming. My heart bled for the people impacted by the destruction. I hadn't planned on staying the night, but I had spent so much time talking and sitting in the shambles with the people that I lost track of time. When I drove over, I had every intention of going home the same day. But night began to fall, and the five-hour drive back home would have been too much for me. I called my husband, Corey, around eight o'clock that night to tell him I was going to stay. He agreed that would be best for me.

As I drove, I was desperately searching for a restroom when I noticed a wrong-way driver driving on my side of the road. He was about five car lengths away when I first noticed him. I was so tired that I thought my mind was playing tricks on me. "This can't be real," I thought to myself. He got closer, about a car length and a half in front of me. Everything awakened in me and told me, "This IS real!" I was so alert by that time that I could see his eyes. They were like lightbulbs beaming into my soul. I saw death in his eyes and knew death was about to be my fate. How was I the only person on the road with him at this time of night? When he got about a car length away from me, I knew he was purposely trying to hit me. I saw him grab his steering wheel and turn it, with what seemed like all his might, in my direction.

At that moment, I felt as if I had been transported into one of those kids' video games. I tried feverishly to avoid him by turning my wheel with all of *my* might.

But, if you know anything about Key West, there is only one lane. If you continue to turn, then you fall a few hundred feet down to the ocean. I stopped the car and waited for him to slam into me, potentially turning my car toward the ocean for sure death. I immediately started calling out, "Jesus! Jesus! Oh Jesus, please help me!" Everything after that went in slow motion. You ever have those moments when you know only Jesus can save you? Well, that was my moment. God was not about to allow the head-on collision this man was aiming for. Jesus took the wheel of my car and turned it so that the man could T-bone me instead of hitting me head on.

The darkness on the outside penetrated the inside of my car. I was having an out-of-body experience. There was darkness all around me. That eerie kind of darkness that makes you want to hide under the covers and pray it away. I was being buried. Six feet under. My grandchildren were calling for me and I hollered, "Lord, I am not done." Then, I saw my mother. I cried out, "Lord, it's not fair!" With those words, I was transported back into my body and immediately regretted my prayer to come back. The pain was excruciating. Like nothing I'd ever experienced. My seat collapsed, and I was trapped on the floor of my Prius. I was trapped in that tiny car, my body racked with pain, living a nightmare that didn't belong to me. After everything I had already been through in life, now this? Jesus! It was like the Lord came down into that tight space with me to offer encouragement, protection, and most of all - correction. Instead of pitying myself in the pain, I began to think about the things that mattered most - Corey, my kids and grandkids, the people I had helped along the way, my church family. I saw their faces right there with me as I lie trapped, numb inside the Prius. And, I was grateful!

Right there I made the decision that if God spared my life and allowed me to be found alive, that I would live my life to the fullest and share the message of Gratitude with everyone I encounter. I vowed to be His mouthpiece for Gratitude. I just needed to get out of the car. When help finally arrived, I was trauma hacked from one hospital to another. They said my back and both hips were broken. My ex-rays looked like a person that was completely broken on the inside. The second hospital, five hours later when they did the second set of x-rays, it looked like a different body. It looked like fractures instead of completely crushed bones like the first x-rays. Miracles, signs and wonders...they follow me.

I only got those second x-rays because the surgeon that looked at me before surgery said, "No, I want to do x-rays and I want to see what the new x-rays say." When the second set of x-rays came back, he said, "I think that with the factures that she has, although they are major, I think she can recover and in a year she may walk. I want to try that." I know he was an angel sent by God. I am so grateful for that surgeon, because in two months, through persistence and the help and grace of God, I was able to walk again.

I later found out that the man who hit me was a voodoo priest who was trying to commit suicide. While his life did not end on that day, my new life of gratitude began. On October 2, 2017, I learned that intentional accidents do happen. There was a reason why I was the only one on that road at that time. That man intended to take his life by causing an accident that could have taken both of our lives. But God blocked what the enemy was trying to do. My Father in Heaven used that accident to propel me even closer to Him. My whole mindset changed on that day. Knowing that I had temporarily left this earth and was brought back to life was all the clarity I needed to set the course of my life to Gratitude. Now I have such an urgency to share the message of Gratitude. I know it's my life calling like I know my mother's name is Alma, which means "Soul." What is so sad in all of this is that two weeks later, the same man who ran into me was in a similar accident against a 16-wheeler truck and lost his life on that day. To this day, I continue to pray for his soul and his family. I found out about his death while I was still hospitalized. His death greatly impacted me because I believed that we both survived the accident, and I wanted to talk with him about how God saved us for a reason. It hurt me so badly to know that he wanted to end his life so badly that he was involved in the same type of tragic accident two weeks later. Here is text from the article regarding the accident that took his and another man's life:

"Two Key West men died on U.S. 1 in Islamorada Wednesday afternoon after their southbound-traveling car crossed into the path of a tractor trailer heading north, according to the Florida Highway Patrol.

Jason Morales, 28, and Roberto Alfredo Blasco, 46, were pronounced dead at the scene of the mile marker 79 crash around

3:30 p.m. Morales was driving a 2011 Toyota Camry, and Blasco was the passenger, according to the FHP report. Morales crossed the center line of the highway and hit the left wheel of a 2018 Volvo TRK driven by Andres Gonzalez Suarez, 59, of Miami Gardens, according to the FHP incident report.

Morales, according to the report, then lost control of his Camry and skidded into the path of a 1997 Mack truck driven by Louis Aguiar, 38, of Homestead. The truck T-boned the passenger's side of the Camry, the FHP report states."[1] For the full article, visit https://www.flkeysnews.com/news/local/article180962576.html

When I woke up in the Intensive Care Unit of the hospital and learned of his fate, I searched for his Facebook page to understand more about him. I saw several posts he made regarding his beliefs, which were very different from mine. His posts mentioned the devil and the occult, and his last post that I read appeared to be of him worshipping a false God. In my heart I believe this man was in a tough place in his life. A few days before his death, he did a Facebook Live video where he gave the impression that he was using drugs on the live video. All I could see was hurt and devastation through his posts and his actions in the video. By the way he appeared through Facebook, I don't believe he knew his own worth in this world. The remaining portion of funds from the sale of this book will go to Roberto Blasco's family because I want them to know that he did matter regardless of what he did.

During this time of my life, I thought of the words of one of my mentors, Brendon Burchard, who also had a near-death experience. He was driving a car in the Dominican Republic and took a turn that would forever change his life. At what he believed was the end of his life, he asked himself some questions. He asked, "Did I live?" "Did I love?" "Did I matter?" I reflected on those questions time and time again after the accident. I realized I had lived. My life may have been full of some great ups and some horrible lows, but I have lived. Only, I knew I still had more life to live. I did love, and I loved fiercely - my family and friends had all benefitted from the deep love I poured into them. And, I did matter. I mattered to my family, my friends, my employees. But most of all, I mattered enough to God that He spared my life in that accident, and He kept me every day during my physical rehabilitation process.

I learned how to think differently, breathe differently, move differently. I learned how to live differently, love differently, show up differently in the world. I learned how to walk again so that when I walked into rooms the room would shake from my very presence. That's how powerful my gratitude for God is. It has shifted me into new territories, new realms that I couldn't even begin to access before because I didn't fully understand how to be grateful for every single thing that ever happened in my life.

I was able to shift from regret to Gratitude. There are two distinct sides of my life, one before my accident and the other after. I can look back now pre-accident and see my lack of Gratitude during this time. But, when I look at where I am today, all I can do is rejoice and think about the lessons I learned in this process:

1. One must quickly shift into Gratitude, as life happens to all of us.
2. Thank God for the pain. I am alive to feel pain.
3. Get into action. Nothing happens unless I put one foot in front of the other.
4. Pursue life with passion.
5. Look at life from the lens of Gratitude.
6. Count my blessings.
7. Live out my highest calling.
8. Endure and do all things with the help of God.

9. When something doesn't go as expected, I continue to ask myself, "What is the Good in this?

10. Embrace everything! He did not need to grant me another breath, but He did!

What are some of the intentional and unintentional accidents or mistakes you've experienced, and what lessons can you learn from them?

Scripture to meditate on:

"And we know that all things work together for good to those who love God, to those who are the called according to His purpose" (Romans 8:28 NKJV).

Homework:

Reflect back to a time when you were involved in some type of accident (intentional or unintentional), or you made a mistake. Write down all of the emotions you felt during that time. If they were negative emotions, I want you to write a positive emotion directly next to it. If it was a positive emotion, then put a check mark next to it. If you have more check marks than you have a new emotion written down, then you may be closer to your Gratitude Transformation than you think.

I so desperately want you to understand that everything you've been through - every accident, every mistake - was designed for you to show up differently in this world. That you would live with such gratefulness in your heart and soul that it awakens something new in you and makes you want to share your gratitude with others.

Chapter 6
Forgiveness

Life has a way of coming full circle when you least expect it. After moving to Florida, I saw the man that lived next door to us when I lived with my grandmother. He smiled and hugged me so tightly. He was so grateful to see that I was still alive because he had just assumed that I had been killed in my grandmother's home. It's sad that people seemed to know what she was doing to me, but no one did anything to save me.

With everything I had gone through since childhood, I had to release all of it. I no longer wanted to be in bondage to my past. I began to release the things that still had a hold on me. I've heard it said that when you forgive, it's not for the other person. Forgiveness is for you, so that you can be free. Through all the abuses I went through at the hands of my grandmother, my aunts, uncles, and my cousin, I was able to rise above all of it. Sure, I had turned to drugs to dull the painful memories of those incidents. I had even had multiple abortions because I didn't want to bring children into a world that could be so cruel. Yet, after sitting still with God and knowing He had already forgiven me, I was able to forgive myself for using drugs even as I was pregnant with our oldest, becoming a topless dancer as a teen, and having the abortions. I was able to forgive my first husband for the turmoil he contributed to the marriage. I chose to stay as long as I did, so I had to not only forgive him, I had to forgive myself for allowing myself to stay. But, to be fully free, I knew I had to forgive my grandmother. My greatest pain was still locked up in her house in the

Dominican Republic. I had to go there to take back the key to the little six-year old heart she broke so that the little girl in me could finally grow up and fully embrace this life of Gratitude. And, that's exactly what I did.

In the beginning of 2002, I had gone to the Dominican Republic to bury a family member. After everything was done with the services, I talked to my sister about driving the two and a half hours to confront my grandmother. We spent the entire drive with me running through what I would say to her. When we got there, I was cordial. I walked around the house, and I remember going into the backyard and seeing the washroom where she had made me wash all those pots and pans to the point my fingers would bleed. I was transported in time, and I could hear her voice saying, "I can't see my face in it, so it's not clean, yet." The rays of the sun were so hot that day that they beamed onto one of the aluminum pans and I saw a rainbow. At that moment I felt such rage and hurt. The Lord said to me, "You can go back and spread the rage, or you can choose to forgive. You get to choose which way to go." I chose to forgive, to let go, to heal so I was no longer bound by my grandmother's misery. I went back into the house and told my grandmother about the love of Jesus. She accepted Christ that day. That's what forgiveness will do. I never saw my grandmother again after that day. She died a few months later. I am now at peace knowing she is with the Lord and all is forgiven.

There, in Abuela's house in the Dominican Republic, I was able to fully let go of the years of pain from abandonment, rejection, neglect, and fear. To let go of those things that were holding me back and learn to be grateful in things that we don't often find gratitude for. What is most important in our lives is that we embrace gratitude. Transformation comes from our ability to be grateful. The things that have happened in our lives are real and true, but the question is, can we begin to start living differently? Sometimes we discount just how good something is until we compare it to how bad things were before. Now that I am on the other side, I can see the good in every one of those bad situations, and I'm so grateful for that.

I encourage you to embrace gratitude. It's through gratitude that transformation happens in our life. Ironically, it's actually my son-in-law that taught this to me way before he and my daughter started dating. He wanted to date her, but she was only fifteen and I said that she wasn't going to be allowed to date at that age. "Why would you want to date her?" He said, "I have a journal and I've been journaling all the things that I want in a wife and she's every single one of them." I was impressed by this and it stuck. I began to write down the things that I wanted. I made a list of all the things that I wanted in a man. I wanted someone who didn't have children of his own because I already had a whole tribe of them myself. Someone who had never been married before. The list went on, and God supplied everything on my list and more in my husband, Corey. I am so grateful for him. Corey chose to come into my insanity. He was the Sunday School teacher of a single's group at church. There were thirty-three women in the class and only a handful of men. Many of the women had not been married nor did they have kids. I was divorced with four kids and only wanted to be a part of this class to hang out with adults. I wasn't looking for a husband. But God saw to it that Corey would be my husband, and eleven years later we are still going strong. This man goes beyond anything I thought I deserved. He's a good man; I mean he's a good-good man who comes from a good family. We have embraced each other's families so easily, and I could not be more thankful. The love he has for me and my children is unmatched by anything I've ever experienced. He embraced all four of my children as his own, and we continue to love and support them as if we had them together.

I spent so many years with the voice of my grandmother judging me because of being and looking like a Mulatta, but now I'm grateful for it. I write it down. Why am

I grateful that I'm a Mulatta? I'm beautiful. I age well. I have great bone structure. This comes from my genetics. It allows me to train and have results quickly. At my age, I am still in the gym keeping my body right. Since God spared this temple, I do everything I can to preserve it because I've forgiven myself for the years that I didn't.

Am I healed, whole, and healthy? Yes! Is everything perfect in my life and my family? No! But everything has been perfectly designed by the Master of my life, and for that I am grateful. Your gratitude journal draws unto you the things that you want. I have witnessed how my gratitude and writing it down has brought to me so many of the blessings I see in the lives of my children and now my grandchildren. The biggest and most amazing blessings that I have in my life. It took forgiving myself, a whole lot of people and even situations for me to clearly move forward with a grateful heart so that my cup continues to overflow with good things.

Who do you still need to forgive in order to move forward with the abundant, peaceful life God has for you?

Scripture to meditate on:

"Bearing with one another, and forgiving one another, if anyone has a complaint against another, even as Christ forgave you, so you also must do" (Colossians 3:13 NKJV).

Homework:

Start a gratitude journal where you will write down all of the people and situations you need to forgive. Keep a log in the journal to record the day that you confronted or forgave that person or situation. You can do it face-to-face, by phone or by letter, but just do it! You will be so pleased with yourself when you see how that forgiveness will turn into gratitude. As you write things down, set your intentions when writing the things that you are grateful for. It helps you to focus on what's important.

Remember, it's never too late to forgive. Forgiveness brings you peace. Forgiveness can restore relationships, break generational curses off of your family, and bring you to a place of wholeness and completeness. Your life can change in an instant through forgiveness and gratitude.

Chapter 7

Embracing Your Gratitude Transformation

It's time to look for what's good in life. Tony Robbins, American author and life coach, says, "You and I are always a decision away from framing our state." We get to decide if we will see life from the good or the bad. It's time we wake up the Giant of Gratitude in our lives.

Tony Robbins does an exercise called "Priming" each day. It's when you sit still and think of three things you are grateful for. If we each took the time to write the three things that we are grateful for daily, I believe the world would be more grateful, happier, and more kind to one another.

Transformation begins with you. If you are ready to shift into a space of intentionally living from a place of gratitude, there are some steps you can take to get there:

1. Change your story, change your life. Don't let anyone tell your truth but you!
2. Leave your faith as your legacy.
3. Do something to help someone else.
4. Tell someone why you are grateful for them.
5. Find time to rest your mind, body, and soul.
6. Get clear on what you want your life to be like.
7. Stay in the present.
8. Get a Gratitude Accountability Partner.

9. Forgive, forgive, forgive - yourself and those who hurt you.
10. Choose to be grateful!

Putting these steps into action will help propel you into a place of gratitude. They did for me. There is nothing now that I will go through in life that will make me ungrateful. I've received so much that if I died today, I would be the most grateful person on earth. I'm so grateful that I've even started an entire Gratitude platform on social media where all we do is talk about the things that we are grateful for. I'd love for you to join us on our private Facebook group called **Gratitude Transformation**.

After reading this book and following the steps outlined, share your gratitude experiences so others can bear witness to your transformation. Use the following hashtags when posting: #gratitudetransformation #gotgratitude.

Zig Ziglar, American author and motivational speaker, said, "Gratitude is the healthiest of all human emotions. The more you express gratitude for what you have, the more likely you will have even more to express gratitude for." This is the measure I use for my own life of gratitude. The more grateful I am, the more I receive to be grateful for. I pray the same for you.

I thank you for taking this gratitude journey with me, and learning about my Gratitude Transformation. It was far from easy, but now I can finally say it was all worth it. I had to lose my life to learn to live, so I embrace gratitude. If you learn to embrace it, as well, and live a life of gratitude you will find yourself transformed.

The Greatest Gratitude Story
Ever Told

The last family that lived with me in California was a single mom with four kids. We got along so well because our lives were so similar. One of the sons, Adrian, has unfortunately been in the same correctional facility, Twin Towers Jail, where Marco Sr. spent his time in jail. Adrian has been in jail for the past seven years for killing a man in self-defense when Adrian was only sixteen years old. Because he was scared and didn't know what to do, he and a friend hid the body. Adrian grew up in the church and knew what he did was wrong, so he went to the church and his parents to tell them he was going to turn himself into the police. He told the police everything. Instead of trying him as a minor, since the crime happened when he was sixteen, they want to try him as an adult because of the laws in California.

I recently went to California to visit Adrian. When I went to visit with him, I learned that Adrian has dedicated his life to learning, studying and teaching prisoners on cognitive behavior because I used to bribe the children with money to read self-development books when they were little. He told me that inspired him to want to do better. He works to change the mindset of inmates who want to commit suicide. Adrian said he remembered me telling him, "When you are good, I want you to learn to pay it forward and live from a place of gratitude." He said he reads 100 books a year because every inmate there comes with different challenges, and he needs to "step up his game" in order to teach and help them. He said he is so grateful and thankful that even if he is imprisoned for another 70 years, he will walk with the Lord and do what God calls him to do. He said he will "live from a place of gratitude and ask God what I can do for the world rather than why did this happen to me."

Before I left Twin Towers, fully immersed in my tears for how humble this young man is even in this challenging situation, he said, "The mind expands, and the life expands." He remembered me telling them this as kids. It was because of this that he said he will continue to expand his mind through reading so that his life can expand, and he can help other inmates expand their minds and lives, too.

Questions for the Reader

In your small group settings, take the time to answer these questions and have a discussion around how you got to your place of gratitude. If you are still on your gratitude journey, that's okay. Talking about it in your small groups will help you discover ways to push you forward on the journey.

Your small groups can consist of book clubs, church groups, friendship circles, etc. Whichever way you choose to design your small group, be sure you create a safe space where people feel comfortable sharing.

1. What are the things that brought you the greatest pain in your life?
2. What about Glenis' story most resonated with you and why?

3. How has your life been impacted by reading this book?

4. Tell us about a time you were ungrateful and couldn't find your way to a state of gratitude. What triggered this?

5. What have you not forgiven yourself for that might be impacting your Gratitude Transformation?

6. Who are the people and situations that led you to a place of gratitude?

7. What do you do for self-care - mind, body, and soul?

8. What are you doing today to help others who have expressed tough times in their life?

9. What can your small group do to support you on your gratitude journey?

10. What activities can your small group do together to bring the Gratitude Transformation to others?

Would you like Glenis to come and speak to your small group about ways you can start the Gratitude Transformation in your local community?

Contact Glenis at
Glenis@GlenisHargreaves.com to
schedule her visit.
Join our Facebook group: **Gratitude Transformation**
Visit us at www.GlenisHargreaves.com

Reference:
[1]Goodhue, D. (26 October 2017). *Two Key West men dead after car T-boned by tractor trailer*. Retrieved from https://www.flkeysnews.com/news/local/article180962576.html

About the Author

Glenis Hargreaves is a wife and mom of four delicious adult children, but her favorite job is being "Glamma Glenis" to Ella, Lily, Bella & David. If they were allowed to swear, they would swear that she is the best "Glamma" there is.

Glenis wears many personal and professional hats. She is a licensed public insurance adjuster and has adjusted claims for over thirty-one years on the side of policy holders. She currently holds licenses in California - where she is convinced God lives - New Jersey, Texas and Florida - where she believes God has his second home.

She is the CEO of Your Recovery Team Inc. Recovery is her business and ministry as she is a recovering addict sober for twenty-seven years by God's grace. She, and her husband, Corey, are the co-owners of Fitness 4 Everybody. She is a fitness competitor and a Team Beachbody Coach who enjoys leading her online team, "Team Gratitude." She is also a real estate broker and owns God's Home 4 U Realty & Investments LLC.

Glenis is an author, speaker, breakthrough specialist, and a Gratitude Coach. She owns multiple companies, but her most recent accomplishment is Gratitude Transformation Ministries Inc., a non-profit organization created to help people growing in their knowledge of God and to empower them to grow in gratitude. Glenis wants her life legacy to be Gratitude Transformation. She believes we all have difficulties in life, but it is the story and meaning we give to them that matters.

She decided, once and for all, to be extremely grateful and transparent about her most intimate private life to be able to help others embrace their own Gratitude Transformation. She has learned that every single day is a blessing from God. She is forever grateful to God for giving her the courage to release this book to start a Gratitude movement like never before all over the world. Glenis believes we have been blessed with abundance, and because of this we need to share our stories of Gratitude and thanksgiving to

God for all He has done. She believes we were born for such a time as this and knows that we are the right people to rebuild The Bahamas in God speed. She wants you to join her in this movement.

Made in the USA
Lexington, KY
12 November 2019

56904530R00057